WEATHER MAKES THEM SLEEP

WOOD FROG
HIBERNATION

by Martha London

Consultant: Beth Gambro
Reading Specialist, Yorkville, Illinois

Minneapolis, Minnesota

Teaching Tips

Before Reading

- Look at the cover of the book. Discuss the picture and the title.
- Ask readers to brainstorm a list of what they already know about wood frogs. What can they expect to see in this book?
- Go on a picture walk, looking through the pictures to discuss vocabulary and make predictions about the text.

During Reading

- Read for purpose. Encourage readers to think about wood frog hibernation as they are reading.
- Ask readers to look for the details of the book. What do wood frogs do to get ready to hibernate?
- If readers encounter an unknown word, ask them to look at the sounds in the word. Then, ask them to look at the rest of the page. Are there any clues to help them understand?

After Reading

- Encourage readers to pick a buddy and reread the book together.
- Ask readers to name one reason wood frogs sleep. Find the page that tells about this thing.
- Ask readers to write or draw something they learned about wood frog hibernation.

Credits:
Cover and title page, © Yves Dery/iStock; 3, © Hamilton/Adobe Stock; 5, © Raun/Adobe Stock; 7TL, © dbvirago/iStock; 7TR, © John_Brueske/iStock; 7BL, © Jesse Walker/iStock; 7BR, © krblokhin/iStock; 8, © Ernie Cooper/Adobe Stock; 8-9, © Michelle Gilders / Alamy Stock Photo/Alamy; 10-11, © Raun/Adobe Stock; 12-13, © Franklin Kappa/KOTO/Adobe Stock; 14-15, © Skip Moody / Dembinsky Photo Associates / Alamy / Alamy Stock Photo/Alamy; 17, © Jan Storey/National Science Foundation; 18-19, © river34/Adobe Stock; 20-21, © creighton359/iStock; 22T, © bazilfoto/iStock and © jacquesdurocher/iStock; 22ML, © GenOne360/Adobe Stock; 22MR, © Oleg Marchak/iStock; 22B, © Jan Storey/National Science Foundation; 23TL, © sefa ozel/iStock; 23TM, © emholk/iStock; 23TR, © torwai/iStock; 23BL, © Studio Light & Shade/Adobe Stock; 23BR, © Mstock/Adobe Stock.

STATEMENT ON USAGE OF GENERATIVE ARTIFICIAL INTELLIGENCE
Bearport Publishing remains committed to publishing high-quality nonfiction books. Therefore, we restrict the use of generative AI to ensure accuracy of all text and visual components pertaining to a book's subject. See BearportPublishing.com for details.

Library of Congress Cataloging-in-Publication Data

Names: London, Martha, author.
Title: Wood frog hibernation / by Martha London ; consultant: Beth Gambro,
   Reading Specialist, Yorkville, Illinois.
Description: Minneapolis, Minnesota : Bearport Publishing Company, [2024] |
   Series: Weather makes them sleep | Includes bibliographical references
   and index.
Identifiers: LCCN 2023028919 (print) | LCCN 2023028920 (ebook) | ISBN
   9798889162230 (library binding) | ISBN 9798889162285 (paperback) | ISBN
   9798889162322 (ebook)
Subjects: LCSH: Wood frog--Hibernation--Juvenile literature.
Classification: LCC QL668.E27 L665 2024 (print) | LCC QL668.E27 (ebook) |
   DDC 597.8/92--dc23/eng/20230710
LC record available at https://lccn.loc.gov/2023028919
LC ebook record available at https://lccn.loc.gov/2023028920

Copyright © 2024 Bearport Publishing Company. All rights reserved. No part of this publication may be reproduced in whole or in part, stored in any retrieval system, or transmitted in any form or by any means, electronic, mechanical, photocopying, recording, or otherwise, without written permission from the publisher.

For more information, write to Bearport Publishing, 5357 Penn Avenue South, Minneapolis, MN 55419.

Contents

Frozen Alive 4

Freeze and Thaw 22

Glossary 23

Index 24

Read More 24

Learn More Online........................ 24

About the Author 24

Frozen Alive

Snow falls to the forest floor.

A little frog is **buried** under leaves.

How does the wood frog make it through the cold?

Wood frogs live in places that have four **seasons**.

Each season has different weather.

Some are warmer.

Others are colder.

Weather is hot during the summer.

Wood frogs have plenty of food to eat.

They munch on spiders and other bugs.

It gets colder in the fall.

There is less food to eat.

Leaves drop from the trees.

The frogs search for a place to sleep.

Most frogs spend winter sleeping in water.

If they stay on land, they die in the cold weather.

But wood frogs are different.

Wood frogs bury themselves in leaves on the forest floor.

The leaves keep them hidden from hungry animals.

Then, the frogs go to sleep.

Soon, the frogs are covered in ice and snow.

Their bodies make a kind of **antifreeze**.

It **protects** their insides from becoming ice.

Their hearts stop.

The frogs do not breathe.

But they are not dead!

Soon, the season changes again.

Ice melts as it gets warmer.

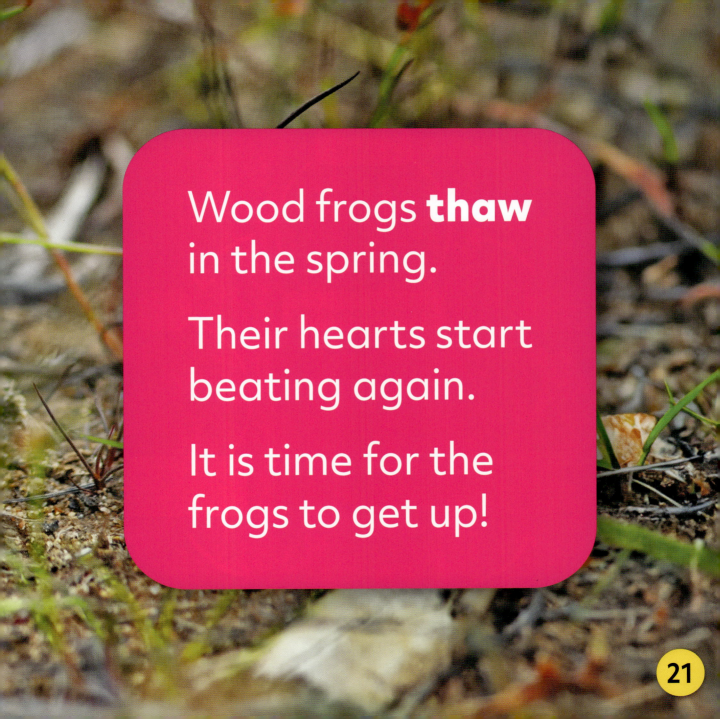

Wood frogs **thaw** in the spring.

Their hearts start beating again.

It is time for the frogs to get up!

21

Freeze and Thaw

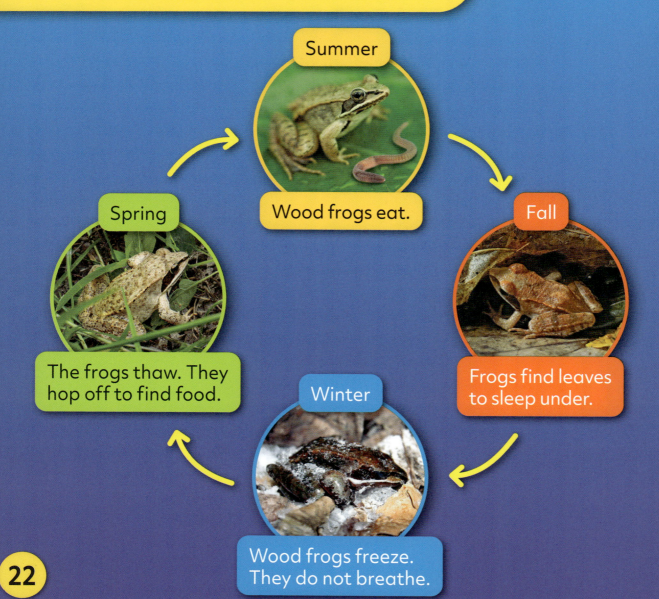

Glossary

antifreeze something that keeps a liquid from freezing

buried covered completely by something

protects keeps something safe from harm

seasons the parts of the year with different weather

thaw to become warm after being frozen

Index

food 8, 10, 22
forest 4, 14
freeze 4, 22
leaves 4, 10, 14, 22
spring 21–22
winter 12, 22

Read More

Banks, Rosie. *Why Do Animals Hibernate? (Why Do Animals Do That?).* New York: Gareth Stevens Publishing, 2024.

Easton, Marilyn. *Red-Eyed Tree Frog or Wood Frog (Hot and Cold Animals).* New York: Children's Press, 2022.

Learn More Online

1. Go to **www.factsurfer.com** or scan the QR code below.
2. Enter **"Wood Frog Hibernation"** into the search box.
3. Click on the cover of this book to see a list of websites.

About the Author

Martha London loves writing about animals! She has two cats. They love to sleep in the sun.